وابتهج الأطفال. كانوا قد شاهدوا أم طارق وهي تكبر وتكبر حجماً. وكانوا بانتظار اليوم الكبير.

The children were excited. They had seen Tariq's mum getting bigger and bigger and bigger. They had been waiting for the big day.

"ماذا في تلك الشنطة، يا طارق؟" سألته مدرّستُهُ. الآنسة سمِث.
"أعطتتي أمي هذا البلح ليشاركني فيه الجميع. نحن نطعم الوليدالجديد قطعة لينة من البلح. وهذا هو أول شيئ يذوقونه."

"What's in the bag, Tariq?" asked his teacher, Miss Smith.
"My mum gave me these dates to share with everyone. We give a new baby a soft piece of date, the first thing they will ever taste."

وأكل الأطفال جميعهم شيئا من البلح.

حم م م، طعمه حلو وسائغ.

The children all had a date.
Hmmm, it tasted sweet and smooth.

كان الأطفال قد تعلموا عن الحواس الخمسة في المدرسة

و كان جميعهم يعرفون عن حاسة الذوق، واللمس،

والبصر، والسمع، والشم.

The children had been learning about the five senses in school and they all knew about tasting, touching, seeing, hearing and smelling.

"كم واحداً بينكم أصبح له أخيرًا أخ وليد أو أخت وليدة؟"
سألت الآنسة سمِث.

ارتفعت أيدي عديدة مجيبة على السؤال.

"How many of you have had a new baby brother or sister recently?"
asked Miss Smith.
Quite a few hands shot up.

"هل بامكانكم أن تسألوا والديكم كيف يتم الترحيب بالمواليد الجدد في عائلتكم؟ ربما تستطيعون أن تجيئوا بشيئ ما معكم يوم الجمعة و تتحدثون لنا عنه." قالت الآنسه سمِث.

"Can you ask your parents how you welcome new babies in your family? Maybe you can all bring something in on Friday and tell us about it," said Miss Smith.

"هل باِستطاعتنا أن نجيئ بأي شيئ؟" سأل بن.

"نعم بن، أي شيئ يعجبك، مادام يتعلق بالحواس الخمسة!"

"Can we bring anything?" asked Ben.
"Yes, Ben. Anything you like, as long as it's to do
with the five senses!"

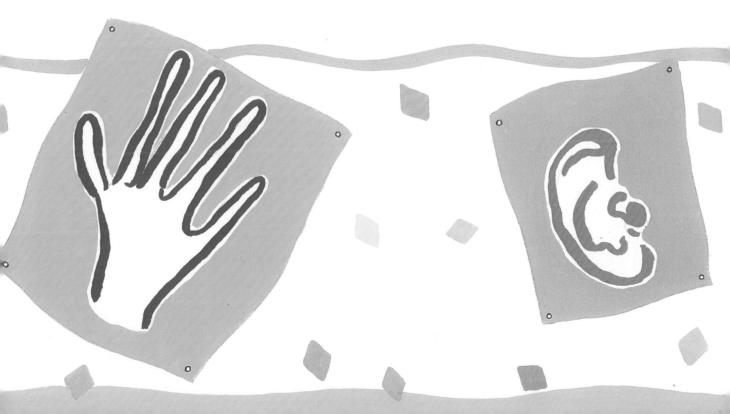

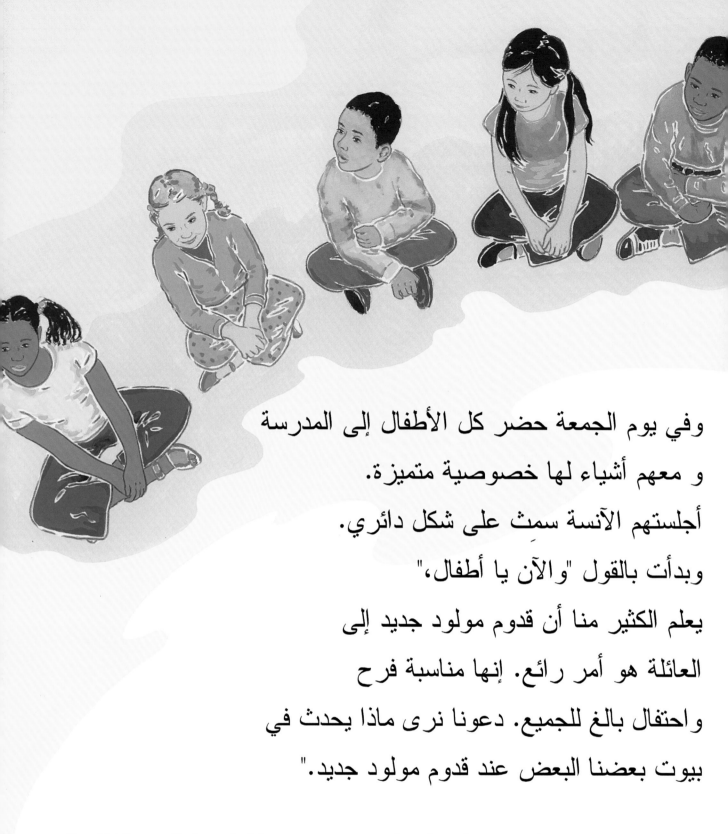

وفي يوم الجمعة حضر كل الأطفال إلى المدرسة
و معهم أشياء لها خصوصية متميزة.
أجلستهم الآنسة سمِث على شكل دائري.
وبدأت بالقول "والآن يا أطفال،"
يعلم الكثير منا أن قدوم مولود جديد إلى
العائلة هو أمر رائع. إنها مناسبة فرح
واحتفال بالغ للجميع. دعونا نرى ماذا يحدث في
بيوت بعضنا البعض عند قدوم مولود جديد."

On Friday, all the children came to school with something extra special.
Miss Smith sat them down in a circle.
"Now children," she began, "many of us know how wonderful it is to have
a new baby in the family. For everyone it's a time of great joy and
celebration. Let's find out what it's like to be a new baby in
each other's homes."

"يا آن – ماي ماذا يحدث في بيتكم عند قدوم مولود جديد؟"
سألت الآنسة سمِث.

وبعناية بالغة تقدمت آن – ماي ببيضة، بيضة صغيرة
ملونة باللون الأحمر.

"So, An-Mei, what happens when a new baby is born in your
house?" she asked.
Very carefully An-Mei brought out an egg, a little egg, painted red.

"هذة واحدة من البيضات التي تقدم بها أبي وأمي كهدية إلى عائلتنا وأصدقائنا. إنها ملونة باللون الأحمر. وهو رمز الحظ السعيد. البيضة هي رمز للولادة والحياة والنمو. إلمسها بيديك." قالت لبراين وهي تناوله البيضة.

"This is one of the eggs that my mum and dad gave as gifts to our family and friends. It is painted red, the colour of good luck. The egg stands for birth, life and growth. Touch it with your hands," she said, passing it to Brian.

"هذة البيضة مصقولة جدا مثل وجه أمي."
قال براين وهو يتلمس البيضة الصغيرة الساكنة.
وابتسم الأطفال الآخرون جميعا.
"والآن من التالي بعدها؟" سألت الآنسة سمِث.

"It's so smooth, just like my mum's face," said Brian,
stroking the cool little egg.
The other children all smiled.
"Now, who's next?" asked Miss Smith.

ببطء فتحت سعيدة ظرفاً صغيراً ابيضاً وأخرجت منه خصلة من الشعر.
خصلة من الشعر الأسود المجعد مربوطة بشريط أبيض.

Slowly, Saida opened a small white envelope and took out a lock of hair,
a lock of curly dark hair, tied with a white ribbon.

"هذه بعض من أول شعرات أخي الوليد التي احتفظ بها أبي
و أمي بعد حلاقة شعره عندما كان عمره سبعة أيام فقط."

"لماذا ؟" سأل بن.

"لكي يأخذوا خصلة الشعر هذه إلى الصائغ لوزنها.
ثم أعطوا ما يعادلها بالمال لمساعدة الفقراء." قالت سعيدة.

"This is some of my baby brother's first hair that was kept after Amma
and Abba shaved my brother's head, when he was only seven days old."
"Why?" asked Ben.
"So that they could take it to the jewellers and weigh it. Then they gave
its weight in silver to help the poor," said Saida.

ناولت سعيدة خصلة الشعر لكارولاين. " تحسسيها بأصابعك."

قالت سعيدة. "انها الشعرات الأولى لأخي الوليد..."

"إنها خفيفة وناعمة جداً." قالت كارولاين وهي تلمس الخصلة برفق.

She passed it to Caroline. "Feel it with your fingers," she said.
"My baby brother's first hair..."
"It's so light and soft," Caroline said, stroking the little curl.

وجاء دور ديمتري. فتح صندوقاً صغيراً.
كانت فيه قطعاً نقدية ذهبية و فضية.
تلمع في الصندوق المظلم.

Next it was Dimitri's turn. He opened a small box.
In it were coins, gold and silver coins,
shining in the dark box.

"أهدى أفراد العائلة و الأصدقاء هذه القطع النقدية عندما
وُلِدتُ لتجلب الحظ السعيد."
قال ديمتري وناول الصندوق إلى راج.

"These coins were given by my family and friends when I was born,
to bring good fortune," he said and passed the box to Raj.

"حرِّكْ الصندوق واستمعُ إلى صوت حركة النقود فيه."
"إنها تجلجل و تصلصل!" صاح راج وهو يقرب
الصندوق من أذنه.

"Shake the box and listen to the sound the coins make."
"It jingle-jangles!" cried Raj, putting his ear close to the box.

تكلمت نادية بخجل.

قالت " آنسة. عندي شيئ."

قرّبت منها شنطة وأخرجت منها بلوزة.

بلوزة كبيرة دافئة وكأن كثرة الإستعمال أضفت عليها الحب والحنان.

Nadia spoke up, shyly.
"Miss," she said, "I've got something."
She picked up a bag and pulled out
a jumper, a big warm jumper that looked
as though it had seen a lot of love.

"هذه بلوزة أبي." قالت نادية. "عندما وِلِدت تم لفي بهذه البلوزة.
وأُعطيت ثلاثة أسماء خاصة."

"This is my dad's jumper," she said. "When I was born, I was
wrapped in it, and given three special names."

ناولت نادية البلوزة إلى سارة.

"أغمضي عينيك و شميها." همست نادية.

"رائحتها قوية وتعطي شعور بالأمان مثل أبي."

She passed it to Sara.
"Close your eyes and smell it," she
whispered. "It smells strong and safe
like my dad."

وأغمضت سارة عينيها وتنفست بعمق. "حم م م م." تنهدت قائلة
"يا لها من رائحة لطيفة لوليد جديد!"

Sara closed her eyes and breathed in deeply.
"Hmmm," she sighed, "what a lovely smell
for a newborn baby!"

وأخيراً جاء دور إيليما.

أخرج من شنطته ورقة. ورقة صغيرة من نبات الصبر.

"عندما ولدت أُعطيت بعضاً من هذه الورقة." قال إيليما. "ذوقيها."

عصرها وسقط بعض من عصيرها على أصابع منى.

Finally it was Elima's turn.
From his bag, he brought out a leaf, a small aloe leaf.
"When I was born, I was given some of this," he said. "Taste it."
He squeezed it and some juice fell onto Mona's fingers.

وذاقتها متلهفة. "أورخ! إنها ؟ مُرة جداً."
صاحت منى وهي تمسح فمها.

Eagerly she tasted it. "Urghh! It's *so* bitter," she cried, wiping her mouth.

"إن ذلك ليعلم الوليد الجديد أن الحياة يمكن أن تكون مُرة.
ولكن ..." قال إيليما، وهو يُخرج إناءً صغيراً من العسل،
"يمكن أن تكون الحياة حلوة أيضاً!"

"That is to teach the baby that life can be bitter, but…" he said,
bringing out a little pot of honey, "it can also be sweet!"

أسرعت منى للتخلص من الطعم المر لنبات الصبر
بأخذ ملعقة من العسل اللذيذ.

Mona was quick to get rid of the aloe taste with a
spoonful of delicious honey.

"آنسة!" صاحت كويسي "استعملنا كل حواسنا،
أليس كذلك؟"
"هذا صحيح كويسي." قالت الآنسة سمِث،
وعلى وجهها ابتسامة عريضة.

"Miss!" cried Kwesi, "we've used all of our senses, haven't we?"
"That's right, Kwesi," said Miss Smith, with a huge smile on her face.

"حسناً فعلتم جميعاً! وسيكون لنا حفلة الحواس الخمسة في نهاية العام الدراسي كاحتفال خاص."

"رائع!" ابتهج الجميع.

وقالت الآنسة سمِث، "وسيكون معنا زائر غير متوقع."

وتسائل الجميع عن من سيكون هذا الزائر.

"Well done, all of you! As a special treat, we'll have a Five Senses party at the end of term."

"Hooray!" they all cheered.

"And," said Miss Smith, "we'll have a surprise visitor."

They all wondered who that could be.

وفي آخر يوم من الفصل الدراسي وبينما كان الأطفال يقضون
وقتاً ممتعاً في حفلة الحواس الخمسة. سمعوا طرقاً على الباب.
"من قد يكون هذا؟" سألت الآنسة سمِث وعلى وجهها ابتسامة عريضة.

On the last day of term, while the children were enjoying their special
Five Senses party, there was a knock at the door.
"Who can that be?" asked Miss Smith with a big smile.

انفتح الباب ببطئ. فإذا بأم طارق مع... الوليد الجديد!
ابتهج الأطفال. وأنشدوا جميعاً " مرحباً بك إلى العالم، أيها الوليد،
مرحباً بك إلى العالم!"

Slowly the door opened.
It was Tariq's mum with...the new baby!
The children cheered.
'Welcome to the world, baby, welcome to
the world!' they all sang.

وانضمت أم طارق و الوليد الجديد إلى الحفلة.
وهل تعلم أنها كانت ألطف مناسبة
ترحيب أقيمت لأي وليد جديد!

Tariq's mum and his new baby brother came and joined the party.
And do you know, it was the nicest welcome any baby had ever had!